COURT *of* THE DRAGON

COURT *of* THE DRAGON
PAOLO JAVIER

NIGHTBOAT BOOKS
NEW YORK

ISBN: 978-1-937658-36-6

Design and typesetting by HR Hegnauer
Text set in Perpetua
Front cover art by Alex Tarampi, *Sigil*, digital, 2014. Courtesy of the artist.
Back cover art by Toni Simon, *Court of the Dragon*, ink on paper, 2014. Courtesy of the artist.

Cataloging-in-publication data is available from the Library of Congress

Distributed by University Press of New England
One Court Street
Lebanon, NH 03766
www.upne.com

Nightboat Books
New York
www.nightboat.org

"Sorcery and sanctity," said Ambrose,
"these are the only realities. Each is an ecstasy,
a withdrawal from the common life."

ARTHUR MACHEN

CONTENTS

MY ASPIRING VILLAIN

nothing jolular at vanim
Villain! jabel violin

JOSEPH CERAVOLO

See your boy ache extraneous, o Queen of Tardis
parliamentary parlor regressive enochian lunch
yawn of haberdashery meadow quiescent to gendarmes
Maldoror or Ubu displeased by lager

See your boy ache like a callous rose in Tardis
charlatan Rome calls unto Ahab too grand
quantum murder abracadabra
sonic Aetna untie brine a bounty to lean on Tardis

See your boy ache is it I whose dorsal fin vacation
inanimate centipede evidence obedient boat
impediment equinoctial leviathan fear

I see your boy ache he'll diminish to vapor
dorsal fin lean aria rhyme Im in
why Nestor bear us citizens assisting Caucasus

Ill encounter comely armada
in simple detail sample largesse unto
violate hiccupping pogrom occasion
Niobe double subpoena Argonaut liquidation

See your boy ache like Frank O'Hara stationed in Manila

Ive been immersed in kind of like a starry system
higher guitar sonic pony innuendo   Plato
wisely abhor the serpent inimical
is that something Ill go muster like rope

camisole one button leery Aeropagetica

Ill tender absorption pseudonym radiant
macho tumor said to be Aquino's
Oulipo Nicean zip code silence   a lucky
Oulipo soon reverse my own pistol

will custody cameras roll? endure costumed wraith ?

why lascivious lyric why voice unnerve

eternal sell entry hazmat Said summons
a Japanese ally emetic rope atavist Nisei aid
a jugular haze today Cortez sell entry

other voice than my own march ransom

troubadour heresy disregard fifty oracles in Lorient

deciduous pancreatic icon, let's adjust furies magic
set dim isthmus dire atom serum
sample old enchantment I lose to most

border company mobile Quetzalcoatl?

sell German battery Propertius can seize?

major key of P, insert nether messiah
Sadat rock Nasser leche you gasp Lancelot, come on!
parables to be soused by at the turn of the tide

whose hand operates the maladroit animal

in a stanchion enemy genus

              tent pole dead-end Orfeo potentate

                    impair new wave antecedent exclaim

Neruda, Vallejo, Stein, Loy, Villa, Balagtas
I spend days counting down minutes to progress
delay delay delay delay
adjudicate idea new rope sung rat race someone repugnant

maybe the grenade seal in front of us
ammonia in case of electric anglo autocrat collegiate
days look over shoulder for crustacean horizon
in the sanctity of our home ecstatic rodeo missionary position

reason why acquaintance Florence

I raise a week long stay in Paris

remember I razed macho Leontes, snow kissed their army

Aetna the masses usurp in sonnet sleeve warp speed

maybe wu ay ni miles at the scene of estate heard hype & question mark
is it near dapple lace road every inch toward Colossus of Rhodes
to monkey subpoenae, pullulate fist & taunt fully usurped
need an art truncheon   I ace neat cycle zealot as if I doubted

equal at least existence delay destiny seek engine

perennial imperfection   increase source of aid

o Yoko o Lima   son of Ezra encode

receive   lore   brazen   revolt   tractatus
Gurdjieff travels to verdant Galapagos

the value of question mark   hoist Seville

nautilus arm-in-arm   unserviceable male pedigree parable

cat got your tongue in Samothrace   lead parenthesis

receding states in the twilight whisper tales of murder

a road they sell, enemy séance neither adore roses

my powers in the morning greater than night

you look stunning this morning, gorgeous, see you tonight

sat in the Alps as all rise up, voice atrocious, I demand
eloquent decree oh yes weave U.S.
I know more Ill eat up security in loss
recuse symmetry Niobe orgy intravenal no clean Hottentot sylph
I know I come to lick the salt lyre day-old Sirmeo relation
azalea enemy Arabian Nights conspire with evidence institute Odin

How are you at work this moment? Are not my puns to be disputed?
at sea, eunuch mince old rope into armrest, obedience
creole I lose you sinister tumescent

want to get good exercise in, a bite of yogurt

wake up longing to taste your blood, wordsmith
come on your stomach lead release, sign hastened, tawny
justice sell a dead-on riot in Salem

I don't fool too sinister in the hour. A little manic, maybe

the same day Ill miss synesthesia, lore, & oracle

why do I waste a day of nothing lunch, online shopping
for a sack of sun owing to a bright nightingale shrouded in
benzedrine

in the wake of mass transit, justice solid adroit rotunda
limits torn under do I weigh myself the task of completing this
poem after hour waste & while you remain productive at a real office

no debt server, no poor luminous question

2

.... : I woke up from a day-long sleep .

I consider each vagary . Much ache probe
A question ensues in haste   eye snot run teary
A matter of soused hermeneutics, a quieted mob less ambient
equal in fortune   , I, to a novice revolver

endure headache. Waiting for you to return
from work so we can takes the 7 to Flushing to join you
family   in   a   celebration   of Ma's birthday at Nellie's on Northern

rise again, let England shake . Command surety negotiate amoeba
admiral

touch yourself in the shower! Imagine open no teeth lick underneath

Im a rodeo-ban nude aerialist of florid dynasty
augur edict via lust & nine angels involve Aegean
Im solely oral assemble to sob inside a well

apprentice swimmer owe inertia romance barricade lie as a vesper o useless I ocean lore cognate Im a quivering rose

& we both ambush some lost, burly, parochial chaplain

My gusts of candor stab at timid mariner as effluvial rattle suzerain adore mild head room

I come supine, while others sabotage art sought as weapon

in the tidal junction , tidal as seismograph of balsamic track

each crystal guard re-side orbit séance once a lost soul jinn

since last June Ive come to receive the Daishonin as tribute

to the life you keep gifting in crystal orbit Queens

someone's nerve always lost to lizard encounter, chast e former hour

I search rooms in our dwelling, laminate passage a sticky wrist
Ill be listening to Polly Jean, brute rope vocable, invert heresy sing
"That didn't need to be said!" crystal a vetted omnipotence .

Here I am quantity fierce sun against konman & cave dweller
animal in care of autonomy sameness like masochism

maleficent appassionato substantive hourglass to brine our selve
I question adjective individual sequence, lore in its tryst

amorous rope invariable reliquary neither vicar nor tender gentry
take summer leave to brine color sedative or sample bold rope future

whose custody souse impressive rope audacious unlace

whose desperation serve morbid gulp I encounter transparent

rope the back of encounter as eruption start venerating retreat
or box under gentry catholic school tender ardency like a
bull old rope imagine stab audience with wild hair virginity

I get so excited when I write, excitable like squid plankton liquidity

Trynisteaser who doesn't think a priori but understand the senses glow
inside punctuation

between world saltpeter, venom pie . Nichiren is the difference

who change what I believe of March , now barricades receive
rose lost in solipsism . A roped Eros Vallejo hastens, phantasm
incendiary Mnemosyne , orison cousin slather butter

What Im dying to say here : why indentation? punctuation where
place sense no lateral movement? who chortle the flow of my ashes
& whose being flowers into fruit through each blanket

I like lazy weekend

I neglect to offer daimoku, for which I seek atonement in evening
greater second experience out of meaning squeeze

I chant for Nichiren to keep yung mga talangkaso, konmen, and cave dwellers at bay

keep calumny & pour motive lore as we erode to Beckett's Cascando
Ubu Rex, Brothers Grimm, Alvin Levin warm the selves .

De-center our home . O rooms I move through blue compartments
while you, Queen of Tardis, push folded boxes behind the couch

I never wished for you to read this , but go on

the life of Henrietta Lacks , & the violent cover-up of history orison en masse silly egalitarian to-do

def-con science recuse key scaffold attitude

versal guitar color sync to a simpering pointillism rope meme import

Vallejo would agree, would argue, rather he'd drink café au lait
than write somatic poetry assignment on tomato surface

Vallejo would rather transcend the need to de-horn Odin

In the best sense goad Essene lead sulk Alamo usury justice
load deposit paradise tribute rope district beer

what bullshit would come out of my mouth years ago! wronging you
paradigm Lazarus between armistice, I lie to self yes yes I do

ineligible valor habitual meme as curiosity

Vallejo would assume the gap ensign pun under Algren

first, I content self to negotiate grudge of a nothing lunch
lore devoured by a moldy equation in retinal rear-view

entrance why salience o lost parent question demise nihilism

I see it lead to despair

a lofty bondage

water boil first thing in the a.m. chant
for peace in Japan, safety of our parents, & security of our detail

who light a match health march on foot sunny rock edge

water boil ignominious unquiet ditch exuberance soon quiescence

cant stand crab clatter in the barrel , same nonce front cousin
who kiss in pairs today equip, at most, to probe gnosis , Moses revival

why quantity sonnet haberdashery Amos n' Andy offend

when I own a pale horse ode occasion Amos n' Andy air nauseous

why Amistad, other zephyr, toy safari

flamingo latent Odyssey rapier hubby nuke
wonder a restless source code enamel
luminescence, Ares mete out de Sade

I try to keep poet in favor of our county to be spoken for along horizon
full of entrances dawn de-stabilizes, elephantine palindrome

ah, Im not a poet to deceive! Solar, dusk-flank, diarist of tally leitmotif

Mama closes her eyes when I read poetry in order to listen to a sober arachnid sequester
in a cabaret, somber pure frontal eruption aria
she sees no stevedore Mnemosyne embrace,   empires away

3

I touch you once, I touch you twice, banjo contrail staccato

Rome a dearer ulcer unwrit   , Atlas Atlas australis

To last us a den of evil, I reiterate my docile armor

suspend hours surfing nothing lunch, the new Wonder Woman sucks

& the promise of the foreign made flesh onto Moleskin, limited edition
does that not set your membrane off?   idem the same

    Galahad I elide

    a pale horse tundra quite discreet

    rear inquiry o travesty kundiman by the condemned

    vain tithe, constellation, quiescence etch demeanor
I hasten to say contrary to empire yodeling

    Algonquin servant velour delay

    Balagtas murmurs "Ill go pour oil" in Catalan

    rear inquiry enemy a European guarantee

    wilt as Anger sings on cue: "Blank Parnassus!"

a name Salvador Dali edit atrium   Ill

content stalactite   .   A crisis? Yes, assume estate

cave in Alaska such telenovela Rabelais voice a deer call

paleontology facial I sing effluvium cudgel

Javier! Xavier! Janvier! Exact music asthma castle
   Nostalgia a mock justice chase by Sisyphus

    sojourn lost Ubu appears sitt—good god—Prim Javier I love—

    Im a centaur whose regime in song fevers at nerve ending

I chant, I delay this moment till eleven fifteen, send
YouTube link to friends, blast the orientalism of its hyena sequel

licorice ring of fire: cylinder a mind slab on turf, kiln
a buttress Toulouse-Lautrec temerity neatly fief, never ill till noon, on the dial

-ing. Tian Tian, the penitent crystal still penetrate Angkor Wat.
Experience, as I void narrator, adapt a spirit Pegasus

Espiritu Santo exhibit Uzbekistan, hydraulic esteem . Redundant séance
assault to dust, lost soul, solace, allot to leaven exclude

no nodding to a naked vista . Europe experience other monument
I define to lead custody facedoom , o sorry extraneous machination

conquistador atrium malade. Laertes relapse . Dungeon habit
degrade other voice , equinoctial hyacinth adjust Niobean

Eden Esau fault. O rose enter , omit lull gossip
eschew the nines. You ought to, visceral Sebastian, add on a voyage.

When savages evacuate, a lone occult sabbath dagger
make a carousel of digit undone, it's a druid eloquence in a hut.

Carousel! Under caramel sundry pine for narrator who is
impossible to dust indigent off pro bono, ya know

5

Back to the task at hand. I divvy up each moment between
these years, : I decide   Id like to spend it remembering

the summer. I wonder not next to you, but listen to cinema
in hazy lyric play backward in a loop , rain slamming glass

I wander into wonder save risk of self revolve
animal question ah apprehend heresy on a dais

A carousel knowledge argue

weather cloud gray droplet outside like April Fool

would never dream to fraternize with banshee, konman, & cave dweller
then, let alone toiletry quiescence evasion,   porous

I suck it up, call Despojado once a week, let summer sun
burn into hard-drive

a bottle couldn't hope to survive the ocean, dilettante agreement melee

rugged madrigal conceive subversive malice entity

sink so low I even blame the sun

I write down the book of levity

it's the piano via Japan Pietro Crespi tunes al dente
via Japan's Saltimbanques allegory

a slipper ferret banjo tunnel

a neat idem the same league

cleave condition horizon chorizo etcetera dilettante
banjo tunnel masala diesel color bungee vertebrae fugue key

I feel like it, that's why.   I hear it, knots to untie.
I view it , books to unbind.

  while you coalesce over the phone into static laughter with your HR Rep
other voice   advance trumpet   revive diesel armadillo

  season of lent Asia advance eclipse

  all my Filipino friends sundry Catholic

  why cesspool gain peccadillo down insect aisle ten

  yeah death parade train nonce to herald lost Genesis

  piano obscuro quiescent ah bleat

  eye count soldier enemy cue

  my assortment murder count as timid Ezekiel
ok I write this so I can slide into hope yeah misterioso

7 HOPE YEAH MISTERIOSO

  alarm set 7:30, fresh espresso brew Americano, my dream
sacred plaid Duchamp record in magenta moleskin, your skill in hand while I

  ready to chant on our behalf. "Maybe with someone you're more
compatible with," you say drifting off to sleep at 1:30

  try to be someone I'm not. At all. Have a nice day
fifty-five high, low of forty-two, feel like thirty-one but actually thirty-nine

my disfigured uncle lead Rome to squander Vienna, sell Argives
for a mil while I access sacaren wheat field,   arid, lost

an ill-observed diorama, lesser narcissist no obscure memo
lexicon erode, no tenor denial

why additional noun, a lot less somewhere elopement enamor delay

Enoch lead Dia where fauna allot seed

queerness a fierce desire Unamuno set sail

season of shark Suetonius alleluia hush meow

innuendo guard yung obscure race mo

dilettante owe effort Ezekiel allow
declension last resuscitation

& the thirst give first, in the morning Vril human

8

in the morning, do you feel like I do—a complete unknown

in the morning, is the language you use lost to shoulder of leisure

in the morning, do you feel cock burgeon caesura declassify

in the morning, innuendo guards yung obscure Erasmus attention profound
              list serve passion libretto

I want to kiss you here, between purlieus parade inferior abyss lead desolate
              speech noise candlelight stupor, declension somber emotion

I see you in the morning light as I gavel gravel

drink under Vienna's last anguish

      my avuncular lodestar

  Im a sagacious villain

          wendigo

              inamorata

          9

   I remember only recently that summer Devil took over ellipses sense
negative capability all euphoria in me

    why did your phone ring mine on its own? Um maybe its cuz you left
our closet door open again, & ghost of little girl asleep there wants to

    remind us to keep it shut? I know it sounds loony, but none more so than
summer when Labyrinth came out, entire month of endure

    hellish heat New York City tear self into full-on possession
mode you hazard séance inferno, ambience in the way torque can be

    save estate river valor persistence

    ah! nervous when it came to the third utterance

    summoning under breath: *Ill sell my soul to the devil*
                                                      Ill sell my soul to the devil
                                                        Ill sell my soul to—

cut off at last second, afraid Devil would appear

in tidy kitchen of obscurity play supplicant

sordidness noun quality nail insurance atelier

noise empire reliquary Dior taint rose

I think it was eight, Ninang in the shower taking a luxurious bath
switch button on cable console HBO to Playboy

something out of a novel by Trollope! but too exhausted to keep writing
itself &
soldier on

like the Devil

10

fuck good Saturday a.m. delay in shower till night
night & you are engrossed in Downton Abbey

more on arousing the Devil that summer at Tudor Towers after I see
communist language iniquity assimilation filial on table

convene, save, equate guitar query insert same-day
bondage Ill brine aquiline avenue, as did Queneau, to whom

sample comely empire humiliate seven way sling proverb,
Nicaragua, Old Europe, tryst

sample undulate cortex, a Medellin coalescence in
rucksack doth annihilate, nonce lasso indeterminate comeuppance ululation

ahh—Saturday

cousin to era of sedation

to commiserate

all my love

all my love

all my love

all my love

all my love

all my love

under banner

YOUR MOM MAKES THE BEST PANSIT

she O.G.

brisk walk to & from the library
as we skip in step take stairs back

I amortize ma chambre, essay memento mori , sing
probably , more proverb if gold rose persist

but I'm hoping to tell you more about the daemon
supplication in my throat

not an issue of whether at this point, but which

11

gaijin gaijin wolverine—-yeah , sky Asano & then Shige
to face Moriko of the Asian Male Paternal Eternal Decree—a tango

why abjure o seven-head dragon in Peru—enter
the void—cudgel penultimate sequence why daemonize sixty nine

eunuch vice—abacus rope odious salt gendarme

12

Tangle in the hour oh seven serpent year you want us
to cajole Oppen's ultimate money sequester Aladdin
all sixty nine vice panic in the senate

yeah Im obscure, but I leave you deep inside the interior

Louvre interior, grit resistance flight jelly

nothing lunch with nobody

bet purse on Pac he's a haole with a family

when you leave for work I lie in bed dream slot
salt & arduous

arduous & salience rose antecedence peg
pegged
undue grit anonymity

in unison pose, urgency grandeur
natural lantern   deciduous Orion

lore I brand force gene under pinion

lost daemons introduce

13

Tangle in the hour admit one
set to zero   jelly   Pyrenees
anoint sleek tunic
slur ratio tone   frazzle linen   Ill acquire hey
a masque I audit ardency lamentation
                    name on the lam
hallucinate Tin Pan Alley seam between redundancy
to chant first light candle no incense
hour later half horn of music chant
they'll ascend to a seizure ninth circle counter salt circle
let go of larger scale
          Why sing ocean multiply into imperial territory
season of nip-tuck, same-day sawdust identity
Ill ascend, a vibrato force Jane Doe
soot & grit, salt undo arduous solvent
chaste authenticity , or undo tremulous grandeur
                    nature de rigueur
insurgent apostasy unanimous dune

14

It's been awhile, I know. Having to articulate the present
enemy hamper ecstasy retardant, denude

why do I not further simplify my life? I delay
rather than allegory process the dust, so when I chant

hours later, no vanity denial why séance question
pardon me, Queen—quite possible hiccup emerge

ahoy emergency question possess adroit taste!
why allegory adjoin tomb I almost aim for

North Star nuance seat rope equinoctial season
pork essence barcode grave deceive less retardant acid taste

to each their own diminishing return, allegory acquit adequately!
why guns do grit who ration use

Hey!, solid leper! A trooper I know whose sequence
devolve into passenger tsunami, a mise-en-scene too

comely to cause adjournment, retardant to dust
sing pregnant gendarme—no, Eterim nods

so don't so don't—Id rather us dance in outer formation
key of cemetery music question endure war of the worlds

dilate like it

15

The cancer bit into quarter vice
Semper Fidelis compliance

nothing tastes like anything, man, when I feel this empty
all day menagerie usury candor brain clownfish

what the fuck do you mean Im defensive?
purity national malignance

sundry look westerner ingenuity late medium noise
whose true form seven serpent lives within . Huh? Tell me whose

solar plexus algae dialysis , I don't understand why
you surrender lost weekend to intimidate perfect dementia

melancholia solid , enough silk net
I wonder how to stop feeling uneasy, red button push itself

much ado saline desert transcend Dutch humor
each nonce a need , each nonce an ocean

vision reprobate little barn over easy
pillar category eminence vision heel

not having fucked so good will put
a hasty trope surprise chance for a system to

rely on heredity, a grayish pumice tangled in our
English. I thrill at any measure against the REAL

reality point rope entrance solar orb pause creosote
pawn lesser English on death row——guns

fire to drug sisyphusian empire, phylogeny-lead
fiscal inadvertence synod Nazi mannequin

pain of dislocation surfeit   loss loom
like apocryphal abolition , hush commons

o nervous ukulele

adventurous Aryan in a coarse ravine

commons dualism East

okay corral o bearer of cancer

burgeoning minotaur silence in the grain, disingenuous
why   somebody   at sea   another mood
reverse ambience civet infinitive

Minotaur . Calla leaf
Yeats ambience period
Mesmer stowaway vice tumescence offertory comb
nonce sidle ambience toy thee rose

Lover, what habit is its version at worst taunt
Barrabas,
Its adequate loss yolk otter
Poacher anticipate indulgence
Enemy, Queen, Listen—soliloquy crescendo
sample gargoyle suit not to renege
yesterday.

Minotaur sample yellow saber to diffuse
all to the good, then, easy segue to Orlando
otter vest neither he nor Vertov squander jaguar
next time I won't even wish you good day

17a

velar nasal enter labial fricative
you slide into the kitchen distance gourd
here we go again I know better not to bother
you are no morning person Vril inarticulate
my nose reveal surety interim you undo
       Edison
clarity adroit Ottoman ankle Lagaan

ah pearly sand Hélas release
letter sunless eunuch consequence
you slide into shower silence jaguar
a madrigal a mare an aery a meme
            in Rome!
saracen field París bone Aegean blaer fragrance
follower mist Suez Dario rose Phaedra
I forge raffle ticket ode upon ardor
change into work clothes comet scent loose
line you draw on ocean bed solstice in the Andes

        "I see why you take showers all day."

            17b

        the mole on my nose is furious
        losing you on the train
        while a persistent fan of this poem
        distract & keep destruction above stairs
        example retina value squander
                Desnos,
        ill-gotten gain Angkor Wat can wait
                adroit clarity
        letters clatter equinox nonce consequence
        meme near de-railment
        check phone to watch time hold me
        you probably went straight home, my hope
        an appeal to early orison Hélas
        in daytime mind hold me close & we
        good morning, good bye, have a nice day

17c

prophetic prosthetic pathetic
prophetic prosthetic pathetic
prophetic prosthetic pathetic

17d

Other days I accompany the accent
a desperate cardiac likeness under
crepuscular tomb denude
surge daze rap adequate audit
fall water equipoise sketch

Torch quill climax stilt
strain over ceramic finish
poke poke tongue tongue neck

17e

you say you want your youth back not having it
when you sign on the dotted line mean until
neither of us appeal the night like toads in water
leap out the moment they seize on the serpent

COURT OF THE DRAGON

Full well I know that she is there
Much as she will she can be there
But which I know which I know when
Which is my way to be there then
Which she will know as I know here
That it is now that it is there
That rain is there and it is here

GERTRUDE STEIN

Ive come back from the dead awaken groggy late
involved in a frontier of probe arreared
why is my levitation so intense I forego nature
Phaedrus question Alcatraz song of occupation
dream of super heroine combat daemons in Queens
anonymous Mesmer post own sandstorm temper
why lead hearth to cliff
a child like ambulance equal sign effrontery
anagram acrostic heat
valve equine solitude
maybe lore without frontier clear
I alternate scene between mussel & cicada
in San Francisco, where cliff edges molder
negate, secrete, predispose question vessel
chastity hard as hearth awake grogginggiddy
vessel eloquence tenuous sequential guitar
maybe heaven before frontier clear
thought question malcontent
this life in Queens couldn't dream possible
codex ascertain priceless jewelry
why lead hearth to cliff
hasten book equate legion cobalt-7
maybe adorn whose bed with book seize
forgery torment distillery lake certitude
boundary needs learning kite luck wind
forage sojourn Icarus equation to solstice
maybe arrive with burrito & corn
no salt worth , corn I help self undo these terror
barrel hearth rib divinity
quadrangle afford Mesmer on rope
True Buddha cleaves inside poem
dada balance Rapunzel why Rapunzel
maybe who insist I read to sleep
divinity entreaty hearth Dia peer review
why dream enfold divinity banner expo globe

search closet entrance
maybe whose width clear arms at two a.m.
why double the dolor bitterness arise
maybe grow old mark pure opportune
hasten ardency knot canard
who bring the daemon carbuncle
how many times must I yodel to counter saltimbanques
cliff edge permanence
hospice tale black masque modal levity satyr trooper
these what I feel fabulist delay harmony
doom to repeat past mistakes
valence exigency a new bed
doom to repeat entrances O'Hara initiate divinity
name your English mine
Alma letter a lasso assurance of soul
numb till English cure

someone's dirigible air melody quiet or why one dune contend Trysteaser
misquote early morning rain poem English mine till numb
flood levity True Buddha no way but each bead
world not throe o' yours no dying note for chosen name
bead inside each think of swing behind their ear
brought smelt English here withhold tank speak hour
mist so you'll never know till hope English cure
she name her silence no letter in white no envelope in aether
leaf together out of sight-line mean
lose wife preterit in patience I excuse wont vaingueness
vaingue divinity head she hold to thank for book
hissy fitted cure for English aorta define fool bewilder late
lore wife patient Iceland divinity in Sweden
no history of violence bleat decade front of blossoming
lore of wife name English another hourglass
please to teach devotion
numb till your English cure
oh divinity tomorrow can may will be a well of joy suffer increase
pound of flesh no hissy fitted cure for allegory name English anonymous intent
cliff edge south of the border west of the wind-up nest
momentary lisp in season of which way English return to name nonce wonder
I have been down this road before we bring up roll of film
now the poem begin

confront allegiance temper taunt occupy disjoint quotient delay calm
outer trooper inside dwelling provision English
English nonce can may will outside history between bucket & cave
divinity come like Stockholm inside ear quiet
quiet time write solid furniture operetta distinction allure
maybe in the morning canopy double back tongue ice again sleep dearly
dearly down hall of science Iceland alight
dream spike annul number matter hum realism
realism longing divinity hindsight ear stronghold globe
globe pose summer aorta light Iceland deckle tomorrow poem
field why siesta ascension
repatriate empathy troll subsequence rope vice seismic why paucity
paucity lets go Leopardi Im guilty like Italy
can will soon always divinity or palm outer everyday English name
name English mine I say name angle please stay
entrances dawn stabilize tomorrow yesterday arrival everyday
everyday chance cliff terse list trace of Leda
Arwen my letter divinity situate their English green
green English ounce altar slur you sabotage frequency
down a well English solder circuit star-lit sepulcher
sepulcher roster longing palpitation attendance quarter establish
ignore song lustral fuel outer quarter expansion
expansion sound tragedy divinity nerve utterance
come on fascicle price ailment informant UN English exuberance
exuberance! o language hyena do you invoke Olson
wild horse tear hope ascertain Spinoza oracle permanence
permanence smolder somebody's zombie
serious when I write Iceland lathe penetration dream
dream landscape troll shunt bird instinct
legerdemain lake Iceland ultimatum Sweden enter
enter permit I language inhabit Sweden
name horse English cure
cure hope quiet time outreach slipper
in the morning rain canopy branch tongue finger climb
climb climb name English mine

allowance English entrance hissy fitted cure for allegory
sacaren wheat field pagination volta harness sonnet repulsion hope
what are you doing inside day divinity
letter in white retail krakooom eye matter of salience
salience like Iceland or ambience language cliff
writing waist into valley not to settle on peak
may be arrival inside jacket quiet time harness
when people speak of marriage summer pose the Ozarks
yes too often sentimental aversion absence why gendarme knowledge
sign dwindle ghost divinity scansion tear heel algae heyday
knot loose site of gold which seasonal ale for English approval
destiny my book allegory capacious frontal lobe
between bucket & cave where English name horse
horse English haberdasher cadence linger
solder decade noise divinity foreground choice
murder valley roll indices
exclaim Trysteaser presence continent under quiet time Ares
Samhain's diary name horse your English cure

toads lustral on dais a meniscus disc a cigar

language hyena Mephistopheles insert ten year version

across swelter New York City UN Towers godmother shower Children of the Corn
        on TV

troubadour vivid then or language hyena collar butcher tetch since birth

just so you know tomato

akala ko yung demonyong tumanggap sa aking imbitasyon & bungy jumped at gigil

sign probe negate detail haven't named divinity English much today less synonym

in essence bar code grave to cliff name anger under grotto muster enunciate

o language hyena sign saber hiss low-grade algorithm lead rubies prince

TV or labyrinth or Malachi or smut or comic books or skyline

terror lament volta inquire why horizon aorta colossus impeach

name English tide return furtherance qua divinity

wake up glue inside horse dream name delight

o language hyena record coral reef couch reverie disappearance

hurricane crescendo or catfish city sublimate English

think of sew logic onto calendar away from canopy egret

name English yours divinity instance relief distend

I can will may know pen movement sling intention under starfish aorta

until Caesar solder patronymic denote antipode sojourner

who am I kidding name English yours divinity entrance midway into woods

midway into woods horse name surrender desist sweetness armor moon
burial dapple latticework
here I go depth of field Roman detention Commodus locate
here where you name English
entrance book-length guild tickertape hearth covet licorice lisp
destiny my book legend hostility shelf your key to a million years
note to enemy anomaly what vow you name there English
how is it I feel today parochial aura labis ganda divinity leather hair up
sweetness creature discernment fleet ocean
divinity invincible embroidery
omen ruin Desdemona lead neutron emotion
pillow book clef coronation inside grand mountain
language appearance phosphorous latex obscurity
lachrymose lachrymose powder Ill argue divinity anomaly swoon

divinity ginseng code Jose can you see alacrity couch arm slung across belly
                    3 A.M.
at Seoul Garden with Despojado deep inside glasswork sync projection
in our grand picture see a magic hour lantern
why celestial aquiline cosmos adumbrate
hearth year decade lore depth of field
road to talk divergence what make up sweetness if you choose it
harp about the nagging marriage pose summer frieze
like lithe align empathy record simultaneity occupy nasal cavity
goodbye crater double pounce why shame desire spool belly
or tongue slip ice again gallop lore solar shutter
mouth to mountain hearth sleep causeway
bet you'd rather kindle or ask for a beer peddle musk
delay armor reserve masculine picayune nothing lunch bag
I know beauty looks to you without need for shame
he comes calling like a shovel sign above sunlit tundra
writ live awareness absorption hemisphere somnolence
as if I don't know outcome letter flight down purlieus parade
relief across cliff languor
lassitude Eshta terror papaya lasciviousness counter ode correction
on paper dream arsenic persist divinity heat a loss of keys
I should was I or didn't I that when could you say so
question name English yours divinity in comics
trove serration eloquence window
song perambulation quiescence anomaly temper
maybe vaingueness clings to old horse tear
how English mine tooth cold livery
reach proposition design deviance cherubim
why sing to me shoulder someone
why shame serenade clang glang glang luminosity
quickness assume quietude mission
name English yours eat eat lisp inward cheek
divinity calm Abel desire kinescope hand

Eshta sigh eighties trace mouthful transience
what dusty furnace in Buenos Aires trump occultist
why somber altitude increase seriousness bead
may be a maze Isle of Wight cloth out of mind
why why divinity Jose can you dance spasm future cosmic heroine

PASTORELLA

maybe regret is sold unlike solitude
ambient occurrence loss of ringtone face of debt
front of double Nadja exit Desnos solo o reliquary
epitome horse delay jade Aetna all of each buffoonery
ocean bottom hearth buffet alien lane wide horizon
name English mine pumice canter treble success
live krakooom empty beach seal pups play while panda submerge
on that empty beach we sit close to keep warm
what do you think dream means laminate under Leda
I feel old gazing at retro transistor radio or your vaingue pout
minus tomorrow simpering lodestar
question name English mine irrigate pause blank space
shoulder only liquidity period skirt length of line
maybe regret trigger comely prison patter Ill recompense
divinity willow west of the sun border to border Iceland
lost in gloaming rose pious trope spoon into pause
squander on the mess of seam ladder onion between book
bald squid dormant idea candor masticate
supple variation outer angelic city
revolve octave sulphur lot oracular street corner
hold up retro transistor radio in beautiful awhile white shirt
name English mine divinity empty beach
apparition horizon April eclipse no rose exclamation owed
yay inadvertent utterance Little Nemo in Slumberland adjudicate
plain old cave monster sample invincible desperation
dose of piety call on creationism aquiline medical error humble salinity
receive madrigal wonder Im arrears
when infancy soon dominion pause quarter lackey
Im a madrigal camper purlieus commandant
kiss me name English yours retro transistor vainguely
sun across day cuisine infirmity why impoverishment
he maintains talk chunky goodbye visit stab troubadour show him the way
in a red-eye flight denial pause only sinister accent

dream of the endless around fountain press to neck
a saucer cup dispute warm bowl of quinoa
Saturday lore suddenly aggrandizing
who dare to name English yours final abattoir
appear before blank space

cant handle valentine fuzz hearth bloat name English mine
jump seat indefinite equanimity
ribald Uther blood indefatigable Orfeo
wind sprint arrival are you
name English Quetzalcoatl
vaingue sling retro transistor radio
nerve story pause hoard cloud split coffee
crab crabs arbitrary brand numb poetry
happy birthday Trace lets celebrate anywhere but here
no more segue you know directly less query bonuses
grumble cant handle return to meteor shower status transistor
sample line poetry wont do
in the seldom illumination glass encased subordinate
handle reserve dear sentence lay down condensation
name English beside you lets play
eat eating mushy tongue ice again galloping
a fusion a quiescent a one trapeze rope crane book balance on insular ball state

name English on dais conduit leg kick
balm belly curve without fate
maybe sinus infection hail omniscience Daishonin reveal
wide space open good combination
avoid trap or meme language
footwork seal round hip tongue ice again gallop
strap to dream shape gnome language moan
King Crab meander horizon clue o language hyena
o Trynisteaser o Buddha name English yours
in baby grand fellation mourning
a longitude book simper nais ko ganito tayo
cooped-up icebox paté bee make honey frieze
divinity can does will stray in aorta vessel longitude bloom as emergence
lost stanza ten seconds suite of noon violence
you can name English yours divinity assist movie nurture galaxy center
incandescence bloom chimney you press into me
name language yours bloom daze conduit
my aspiring villainy shape-shift perimeter no progress issue
I bear these lives nineteen centuries melodic gravity Trinysteaser the
        Daishonin
terrestrial armor lead phosphorus endurance kiss bite or trial
day volta month rose divinity caress
my volta slips second
green inside languor wonder emergency the poem
o language hyena ice again tongue gallop nestle bloom
let me kiss bottom lip sulfur conduit twice the rose
o nascent Trysteaser name English mine
divinity guitar yours period blank then space

today rise from bed without spirit kindle your computer
again tears call to the door begin to fall on the board of twenty
tired of all go to the kitchen find something like eating
light the TV command chain much as you change your growl
only the kidnap practice with it all kinds of witchcraft
Ill take anything Ill go to the salon
you are jealous
I hate
not thinking maybe one day someone decide arrebatartelo all but it did
because you see they had everything nothing valoraste
when your kisses were not theirs as I remember it was you not his
today it is no longer cry but admit yesterday I never once thought it

melody in ice bearing volcanoes cities envelopes
to return English mine means whose language
immobile pacific vidriic prenatal
maybe I am wrong to seek out divinity
in the immediate touch like air without which I couldn't
dust to dust or lost soul solace
pure Abel inhuman friar in the Andes Picasso occasion
give up pan de sal your seal of approval or dance to it
name my English extinguish

13

gyre Lucifer in heaven paternal delay temporal
easy affiliate why say perverse reliquary in haste

flamenco dream desert us.   loss our aunt gendarmes

what are you doing this hour weather temporal

my problem is rope, aquiline point without explainable supplement

concede sweltering heat gestated ah well you fill it

voltas why voltas

Ill corral on Saturday

centrifugal letters to each other in secret casing

SEQUINS

secret sequence Quetzalcoatl once exclaimed

back by ink during nothing lunch vowels open

reminder to cross ocean noone hears

I gleam in red, you undress in white preterit

studio of alms I hasten to reserve endure

gonna write you a letter   destiny my book hostile shelling

as to the matter of my patience
vegetal sordid inutile pure as the day kisses your shoulder
surrender vanity mute archway light behind ear
maybe of week distend ocean bodhisattva temple asleep
you feel vulnerable like plumeria with inscription
who compose like supreme ambivalence
take part in delicious ingenuity commingle in story
why sing Apollonian guile
or stab waste resurgent ventricle quantity
inquire song engender sign replace wreath destiny acquiescence extremity

as to the matter of my patience
vegetal sordid inutile pure as the day kisses your side
loss of language denude narcissist inquire envelope
surrender vanity mute archway light kisses hair out of day
easy double introduce extreme Dadaist
Ill corral it on Sunday on Sunday
inquire into October distance ocean initial chase
may be of week distance ocean boddhisattva temple asleep
mind rattle inquiry ultimatum handkerchief you dont salve
grime inside hemisphere head of consulate indentation
not one day since we bee-line outside gallery
flood eternal armor Inca tangle in the hour
you feel vulnerable like plumeria inside handwriting
who compose like ambivalence
take apart delirium ingenuity commingle song
why sing Apollonian patience
why involve exclamatory adventure quandary reverse demarcation
no question maybe you liven night muddy sepulcher
I stab waste resurgent ventricle quandary
burial tender certain similitude
harap-harapan sutra
waste dirigible when all I seek to write enacts dance
delay plaid estrangement leave your mind too macho
inquire song engender sign while I or I & I replace a wreathe destiny acquiesce
        to secede

its wonderful Ive been inside wrought steep delight
its wonderful Ive been invited deep fried
would would you damn would near damn name it
would you damn near wonderful been inside
its beautiful Im sorry Ive been invited deep delight
would you would you Im damned
would you could you we're damned
beaten drums beaten drums yeah damned
oh no its wonderful Ive been inside lithe steep fright
its wonderful inside delight deep tide
damned baby damned baby would you
oh would you damned baby damned baby damned baby oh
dance dance dance dance dance dance

down from pale horse , questions begin , requested stammering begin period

ah your voice entry when you ransack a cadre , venal , dicey

down caballero road indefatigable rope abacus truncheon

you stood at a distance under arch entrance while young Europeans intended

around fountain , tanned , delicious , musclebound , lithe , equipped with sharkskin

cold breath seize a beach face open own feet package of your mixtape

five days since arrhythmia simpering keeling numb, I can appear in poem

relinquish , relinquish , must avail of ode

fall animal guide rise a loss of some eponymous letter

calamity nadir shoulder naivety need signature discovery

made to feel closer even though a rose involve more summer

pursuant to all appearance Im a sucker for the cosmic ruse

certain ration envelope Eden today a wave chasten over meadow

to stray behind left ear

did you amass question familiar to enumerate the rose?

certain paths will stray into a sequence obstruse like an ensuing monument

chance, or it chose us, o serpent inimical

despair despair hail corner horizon

a denizen fault one yacht circa ocean paralegal feast insular labor

poet the ocean no one listens to but know in their hardship who owns the secret

o language hyena senescence blossom

inside but at a comfortable distance illusion can turn indices

name English mind fingertip mouth

poet the ocean secret listening party inside hyena knowledge

maybe October Ill see you pincer assume hazard tear

name English mound Hades evade velour patriarch

resign why name English moon origin relinquish

maybe inside hyena dwende inducement language

its good , period gulp lion Empedocles shush meal

brutal Nestor undo quality

I trust you settled into coyote den

a nude storm prima facie illusion for everyone , divinity

what enemy march question imported

my adulatory identification ellipse reverse question understand dwelling
thrilled you discover equipoise on balcony overlooking cliff
three years clamoring for silence like it
decay somewhere else , some nonce easily lost
rose ruins why trope Circes Ill denote linear columns
my unfortunate habit feet out the door
an appeal I mountebank like musk
germane alarum by a sybarite from Parañaque
ancillary spacious chestnut brown gaze to pour wine over cabbage
iniquity mother adumbrate
no guarantee Ill charge Eden respond stock perforate
Im sure the gallows head raconteur my English toward a desperate meadow
where, a sickle untied , troops on pale horses
lead crescendo on evening like this give up elixir for you to divine

it comes to pass I could relax exhaust

couldn't render epithalamium for Eshta or Memory from the fat of experience

but to offer Neruda in its stead ought to introduce such southern divinity to
      the poem

in truth Id fade in the mist of your stronger existence

maybe I choose to live here like a bioengineer

unsettle voice make who can breathe latter

name anguish mine

why plunge knife into hearth

Nietzsche descend from Calvary

lead crescendo evening like elixir

eruption in Collinwood

name your English mine Daishonin listen to the ocean

empty beach Ive come to ruminate fear I thwart

amass question to enumerate the rose

sensualist bullet wrist

match-flame inquire later orb delirium

ladder when we speak Ill strike question mark portal

torn equivalence sundry ambivalence hold

thirty six hours in NOLA burial sympathy nostalgia

duty legion pause

relinquish origin vivid horizon reassignment

in a good place pushing you all ways

so that by October hope despair ration to heave one

solar moment sequence obstruse

why why fault Cassiopeia in the nude

numeral familial question

name English yours justice or divinity or Tamalpaís street or daze

width speech I hate if community workshop it to breathe

hearth lean apparent coeval Erasmus period

another vane to point hunger

calamitous song opinion for seltzer

wild animal nadir if I choose justice or divinity or this wine

it comes to pass skin tourniquet vaingueness Ill fumble
wander seventh avenue broadway victory crispness your picture context
why pace appearance lone solstice quarter question subsume
you may catch me in a light taut adrenaline rose eternal continent
how wild you let on emperor ought none entreaty troubadour
do you over-determine romance in case of evolve soul sojourn
Parañaque weeding revolver otherness skirt pale horse
why squander salvage die question irascible landing
trident keep breath to a minimum
while you dinner alone overlooking coyote cliff
do these to selves
letter singe numeral alone
firmament Ill annul question separate
Vancouver intersection blessing by massacre yeah
you cite inseparable comment my arrest
Alma gut Debord
Alma hand length of cord
supine in your bed open floor room samba
I wonder
will October revolt against the uncanny wish-maker
did you dine on more strawberries after we spoke
I feel dumb
Please read this
when I memorize your home for a lesson I won't rent
leave this clumsy fool who buoys you
emit case Im a rabid passage confluence lead supple later guest
like an article of time pause blank space
why stop to admire the Jordans in the window as you explain my poems back to me
like an article of time passage in alley under lost city eye bear volcano
terror portent allay
rather not know your night
but Im happy we spoke destiny a lit segue allow largesse
server to mystery gaze as I erase a dosage

Parañaque Ive lost you
unless settee atone for quest as a guide
cinnamon dwelling in our wine
calling the carnal separating rose

21

but to film in that very room

like article of time passage alley under lost city eyes
amanuensis lore period gain painter being
I know which spite of self name English yours convict
inside melancholy marauder colony manacle chorus
willpower pales Ive been thinking about forever
why animal asphalt oxidize immobile hindrance
comment on viral incessant lease destiny synapse
no protest today for P, justice or divinity
just laundry with seventh gen biodegradable excellency
or seats at the table of underground completion poem
Amy Goodman rarefy second system facedoom reality
overjoyed to hear will this mean freedom to ruins
but I hate the west coast legend
jelly of punitive decoration under zone rancid decay
grand marshal armor loom jealousy platitude sovereign
decay impossible period space
rumination atone murder wise sobriety
weigh kiss your hip pelvis
sweat relinquish across divine space

sky pumice decoration zone adieu

nervous textual about my nose

you are full of praise

Peter Pan de sal rope grand armor soul shield us under platinum torso

May day impossible for those who can't forget bereave nor afford pay out of
        day-to-day

ruminate undue murder wise sobriety

Ill whip up twenty jokes on the Sunset Strip

relinquish undue notice period space retroflex measurement comedienne

name English mine according to miasma rope bastion space

rush theater alas lead taste event pause lost antinomy hasten quietude

let me kiss you

Circe ah

why El Greco lead tedium why gibbous candor inquire table brand period

why no sound masque lasciviousness docent Horace decorous

maybe who once obfuscate my sigil quandary

maybe precious pause de-brief

crenellate libertine Eden minion allot Bastille left indentation half a hive more
        to taste 'em

24

Macpherson Lake County tape attached
mind before restlessness construction gavel police siren breeze
I want
bottom lip squeeze crown undulate English
five seconds to vertiginous inamorata deicide Lethe minute rainstorm
quell obstetric why feed lisp emote sea urchin allay feral entrust period
blank space name languish mine I hope winter out who decide what world this poem's
    lore
verdure, esteem, hell, creation detain, despair why an ill-conceived panorama knuckle 'em
    to taste

25

"Are you gonna take care of me?"

impossible to leave probably
name English mine verdure estate courage without drowning semi-colon cranial
plum perch door edge of live votary sortie unsolved
sedate me, Cupid! retain lost spell city ordain eye pause key nebulous suspect
my team just tied the game with six point six seconds left don't mean to ignore your entreaty
to turn speakers up when you plead confront me
a job dash why you quit supervision
occasion to rapid succession
why you question plenty armor period space distance
you were about to pursue come here I wanna talk to you about something
you press & pursue your abscess order
elevator song altitude dream coma

       Why won't you take care of me Where do horrific dreams mediate color
sign riotous fresco entreat period Rome adieu Oh voice I should
adjust equinox present painful exit grandeur cabal nuance Didn't I
tender your infinite entry Quietude leniency unite by U.S. cavalry Minstrelsy
passion under macho curvature A cinema gag or grand guignol costume obeisance
Doesn't trust retardant dimensional period space end of line

Hey   Man-Up   You keep misrepresenting yourself

         Arrear

November open cage   Are you gonna take care of me

    What if something were to happen to me   How about you think

      Stop making excuses   Painful exit

     I cannot take anymore

   Do you want me to skip town   to comb around

painful exit   where's Monty

take care of me   because I take

                    good   care   of
                                                        you

not too hot about seizing your name
August comes to rock corollaries to coral reefs a saintly Capitan Tiago anonymity
ode surety disingenuous you stow away mise-en-scene commodious dandy
how's lunch today feeding its best I keep self limited communal okay
can see self trouble its notification over justice a fine mess
a modular army enter noise bender utterance Landover
problem of anticipation delegate someday falsehood synergy period
indent aspiration villainy ochre auteur piece together
flail impossible in time to withdraw surge tonsure ancient suite
if I see you in those glasses again devil or Abyssynian sequence
despair patois garlic
repulsion. white. shortbread. a bathing indices. frost expiration by a million yolk.
....& then sleep . swaddle the pillow with flower gesture dream month
side-by-side like a feast of sainthood assume millennial facelift
aquiline flash bottom lisp harried shop dynasty
justice or divinity or just fine . name English mine
we quarrel without stating its truth dirge adjudicate trash edit
cue on par with nonce message rescind gain under salad glance
torment as decor a quarrel wheel before period space
its calm like a lake might eat but wonder about eleven later
as if murder immortal pause expand accent first person
I see one pause three character sibilance between vowel
neither one alone nor ode without article to its name you feed
Pre-Socratic typeface order cushion jacket length to scale their destiny thermometer
question black & blue head do I really have reason to complain about magnificence
line set to awake in Sunnyside? no paddle caterwaul in dolorous declension
tell oneself they can wake up uncertain on a bed with frame under comforter
oh something like lute in the grain
pause blank space alert huevos rancheros dinner
indent sign pause pneumatic testimonial here sibilance between rose

HOW SHE COULD ALL LET IT HAPPEN

I break horse & super moon pic . iced coffee . weathers horrible the past week.
you get to a point in mind & body when the eight winds don't sway you
you're welcome it was beautiful today follows the most gorgeous sunset
lion tusk diaphanous question
fuzzy logo ambient existential crib sameness affect injection memory
great dinner at Charles & Susan's told them about violent affection recordings
how I write several books at once & don't think twice about it
do you
story engender eye south mandatory plasma underwear formula Demerol
justice or just fine or Pliny's ecstasy
pointillism oh sorry dispose errant lotion transit volunteer
for today lost centuries measure distance appear tincture
same city mass density translation relation   Tagalog origin
for dance . or justice . or divinity. English, Coyo B

if only I could be green as you
are due this avocado shake

MOTHER'S DAY

"the shows here all fights are prepared by women"
evening at the bar below
only four ninety nine
that's cheap
as we walk to our room a hundred feet away
Id taken photo with a shirtless Pac
about to warm up for his battle with Bisping
anything goes
I say to Bisping "he will mishmash your face"
working behind Atul's lead & one other's
later inside room give Taija a huge hug
I think it must have been Arun's room
or
another minimalist orange variation book by Casey Anthony
feel or leave bleeding through margins
a French door to let cooling breeze certain sway
crystal night
I could swear more people Im familiar with & trust present
it has to be Mama whom I correspond with or new letter I read
cry out name of anyone close to me in their strangle house
whose owner Ive made my acquaintance
name English evening in this outer sphere
when alone you feel the cloth down your back like the cosmos
always admire the poet or comics able to bring bone essence
unwrit till name language happen
get leaves behind in open living space
where owner my family wife with this book in orange flower
"Beautiful!"

plan to meet on a boat but no clear idea what meander

they'd been waiting on me to dress up for photo

here we are on paper boat sail down flood walk

how do you control speed while end doesn't come

determine to swim further downhill large pirate sail

       weigh

to swim but in pants shot punctuate what learn you

ok pick a spot green surrounding dock & city plaza

no guidance what True Buddha force

you'll drown inexperience swim

like stone tread underwater churn to flee

my hand time right so grab it

pull you up birthday suit

who's that young guy in a taxi & suddenly bionic mother in garters

prior to swear your dress

double dosage November a large procession forest giant join us

why fear October disapprove water for three weeks

finally occurrence year desire until wariness follow weather through night

can't see past inch taker at reception of Eshta & Memory's

can't watch Tremé cut too close to bow

happen like winter Im devoid

toads can't wait to seize

double its dose Trynisteaser sadness remember anew
slack Ill write door around period blank space
present sentience lead miracle space expansion bruise
wont for slide sample tongue meadow to entrance
carrot cue nude Romulus voice outer calm
decor a cliché service fantasy deaf unto
limit of flail no longer justice or just fine or divinity
can't see past address reception of Eshta & Memory make English mine
converse sartorial blanket coronary compost salary
outer head lassitude reason commotion
sudden limit felt deaf justice fine or divinity
purity ferocity interrogator
Ill make Z's dinner no problem show up to Emma's opening take off at hello
lost once friend & maybe matter salutary knit selves
voice outer phantasm calm pause blank space crucible
somehow detection
how hard is it to drop that
Latin crusader needles period pause
frond panther question beige courtside dryad word electric
to come to this placemat threat weeks fall without you in bed
how to equip self
gesture folly brass moment through torpor
Ive come back from the dead vegetal sordid
cant see past other head laser reason disappearance green water three weeks
you gotta leave it on like rock ape
or rush to hotel room for another glimpse of head of Vercingetorix
why wouldn't you go out on deathbed

HEAD OF VERCINGETORIX

lie flung back   indifferent question burgeoning courtside
suave rosy mien entrance
solid calm repose under shrug nerve ending
sing record of enduring fiber
what uncertainty orb Eros becalm
enamor incapability commons deign innumerable notice
in crux add pause coursing need set elation then crusade
grip queue onto English name it what's mine wingless

do right by last night
even tho excuse sound like it
sit down for gongyo in fool compassion
instead of heading into bleak evening
seeking hell
howl
hear you with both ears to ground

it will end in tooth if put to wrist like beach
not sure Ill meld
silky glang glang accolade realm of presentiment
I do want to see you Coyote
to subsume, ambush, nonce dear assortment bomb rosary
period to last inestimable fireplace
Im sure someone else arrival to sort eldest ember
novice renunciant use up double docent
why push light to round out dusk
name anguish or just fine divinity
past tense of inside
can we speak tomorrow I mean this morning later tonight
a jitney leaves indentation smolder
Papa sokay a little stiffness from the crash
can might be write off thankful Micah not in car with him
must sound like excuse though
spirit hawk low across cliff
in midtown bar where friend pours neither
one of us emerge behind smoke
steeple terror hold you close when I sleep
incapable meek idea allure pause disappear
incapable leave twice Parañaque question its son
despair why detain passenger through capitol
I own decimation column aquiline ventricle pejorative
sing the gut lover coast name English yours job recourse
ardent equipoise adumbrate demure period
quadrant able to catapult pause why eloquence aria crescendo
but you appear intensity eye atavism decorous bountiful innuendo
song matter liquid database direction
cause effect name English yours equality tonal range viscosity
despair yes lip service astronaut cord acquire pause
oracular encounter rose adore coyote page appear tall in song
same pause appear question force aria
the brown kid at last to be continued batten

WE BEAT IT UP LIKE GORILLAS

yes to be continue
same day hours go to spend city sunken
you exact neither wave across avenue in black
remember correctness hand hopeful
slow along fifty third crossing sixth awareness sunlight
overjoyed
sorry to be occasioned by visit
foolish to send message to meet you still funeral
now that I think about it you skip out on ceremonies since you aren't chosen
maybe you were dying to see me or feet bear pavement less
your right shoulder do what I think
cut above knee how Holly Golightly I said she's my girl later cross fifth
leave re-enter cafe to change outta feet
beads anew can walk dont wait in line let's go
look its Central Park sige ba
what am I thinking its all good we talk about your old one
whose first question has to do with your new
white or not I shut up know one aint wrong to wonder
quadrant mark detritus anneal pause calm squander
        talk talk
armor establish fault line flicker liquid easel accent over surprise
calm quadrant sleeve in situ dwende appear blank space
delay melancholy for days we are here together on trial
reliquary gustatory Ill acquire arachnid zarzuela
didnt you samba at one point this man under shade & that
induced demure Ramses under martian moon
song Ill honor anew calm as purlieus parade
at some point Ill need to go but not before I listen to the ocean
baby extra pass pattern rectify inevitable period endless solar radius
why such calm diversion somewhere pause lost umbrage
record deciduous calm along fifth till garden shift
down Madison left tell you maybe she'll end it
yes we sing lower register test our gaze squeeze toward horizon

count circle why am I voice in rain on bright day
cant hold that but Ill sit next to you on these steps
friend's birthday a sweaty hand off count circle again in October
your shoulder when it's crisp

there desire accident palette singe proffer hearth iota
pause rinse noon call rage orgone
stammer equator deep July
attention suntan towel expose blade nonce audit
two layers salt mine advance
deduce infamy   sell five-day delay Tardis period levy intrigue
cup under tercet   lapel incessant period
levee mass stank   barren
make small incision
salad of grim ale laughter animal east of endless
grab what August scene march nude exit
seize delegate anemone fist en masse
why shrug allegory why sing hatch grace vase period ah
ah ah sunless   cadastral column echo
eloquence puddle assent genial mystery ability
grand tabernacle song reel calm ah or rest Im sure
lava song effluvium contest binge pause
faith noting waver plenty
Ill board the one sepulchral flotilla Ill serve port undone
the green will eat you
respond deciduous kiss redundancy luck moist song list-to-starboard
rose quantity part Oedipus appear alphabet
rose Ill encounter absolution calm space arms clasp lick
rose Ill roam eternal Alma blanket astral pure as animal cipher
alone under gamine brute Aesop emote induction left until de Sade

You can count on me.

39

You win again.

what noise busking romance voluminous contusion
declamation lyre reversal
hour ensue inverse knowledge witness rarer monument
no fight you cant fight Ill manage erudition of pie
indecent question inconsolable sequence to atrocity
no life on earth nobody to see through
name your English mine statuary composition analogous to febrile lane
break down ounce by lone animal nuclei tremble
solder omnivorous lead dose vibration surgeon delay philosophy
no life on earth you win again contusion as dawn fits satellite disc
count sojourner gap
hatchet in hand undone ache local seismosis
in funeral dress justice or just fine or divinity to pull off
before we tear assortment rotation lore
dispute ode escalator   quarter invention
there's no fight you can't fight   require ocean
let's be adieu or platelet of tungsten calm
contract solemn obstacle ecstatic   loneliness period
I'll name English yours for the win

It takes a long time to become young . Today the sun rose, lead us out of despair, conquered envoy odd enough calm. Remote cellular cummerbund, why come from Berbers?

Praise Nichiren today for bringing me into union, grand celestial under Aldebaran. Not since I enter the question, yay o Queen of Tardis who prescribe beneficence apple . Anemones revive first letter, sold forth in voices pause equal to salt benediction causeway for murder . Serrate despondency! When tenuous quarrel stretched across sheets, quantity liquids aim actual ideas semper fidelis one stares most into. Come stare at me. What internal barren cause stolen hyacinth an essential cemetery.

Ill import vinyl altar calm, a piccolo period journeyed sonnet lean coagulant. Consensual . Docent. Escalator scalded in horizon enter frustration , its been hours of delay delay delay, now this pious calm rope pavement sandals to vacate tongue.

Why tremble most advance the hour help us . Question save us inside of almost lexicon pendulous pause o yellow flower Hermès crusade against period blank space. I can please you too if you let us let us be cheers, to these fucking years lets go

43a

serpent inimical Colossus solo entomb mania excerpt
why such Dramamine? Catullus entreat out of curiosity

43b

in my parallel universe discover Im a father of four
in my state of inquiry I base Eden near a lake
unwed to bountiful other whose skin aint exotic
Eden seraphs once at the lake enter adroit

hijo Im a saber she remembers succulence dune I dread column
rolled sand on amazement belly calm city obscure grin sow
since childhood I enter advance lost succor flay soda rope leopard
I drown my nothing lunch in a sack of sun as I enter
listless mist, carried, at last, at last, windowless
be patient hijo the knees are old scent switch fatalism
touch hand uneven why simulation masses reciprocate tendency
policing the quotidian practice sign of the serpent pause blank space
why sign reverse Pre-Socratic alphabet in custody

Call to ambient calm crepuscular futurity
why recollect arrear only intimate contact illicit seed
under galley of social sigil robust vehemence imbue suburbia
suburbia I meant, hijo, to invade adjudicate
sepulcher coupling my window mitigate solaris
boom boom water huh a pocket imbibe orphan tongue regurgitate
destiny area lap to heap here, hijo, a bare screen equine to wristlock
boom boom, hijo, boom boom

why do I experience precious time as spend
hunker down turquoise drop
I remember the back of your head
receipt no arrest I lend you my voice salon encounter

JUBILATE ORFEO SE INTORNO EURYDICE

zookeeper killed by wolves in Sweden
beside the beach you take me to watch baby seal pups
it's your birthday, Coyo B, maligayang bati
sleep comes over me
make it through gongyo it's noon
lean into salvation innocence
nude turquoise pause blank space
your subject head cinnamon rule narration suture
destiny book hostile shelf
you've reached a quarter century as is the case of parables
your verdant hand recede
lore as bridge barter abandon
lore secure senility triumphant
why Ill message you somewhere transcribe Vril stanza
appear in adjacent room pause blank haste divine
not on your birthday, Coyo B! I want you happy
sorry to vanish
why sing a solid identity sauna clamp
HOY! your foot on the gas pedal of my Honda
too demure to speak
enter dialect ocean seismic Port Said
it's probably too late to catch up
October
I mean a head of violent arctic squeamish
despair nonesuch appraise no way somatic atlas
or that beach we gaze at submerging pandas
in cold cold ocean
I leave you
where cold can't recover itself
outer engine portal corridor
HOY! COYO B! establish announcement
nerve of Rome counter Adonaïs imaginarium
lead ulcer a dull terrain

today you appear in adjacent room, viceroy finger in place
marvelous period pause blank spate
much to relate about our visit north of intention
tell me, love, pondering the leaves

have I triumphed   ? averted elastic blank space
name English yours why question actual nonce resurgence
so its come to pass no skin turn inside out no vaingueness Ill fumble
digital gradient set lexicon element rare art Samothrace
one radio listen ellipses equestrian
have I triumphed other than counter nether conjunction
happiness imbibed through weekend variety triangulation
oh exhaust osmosis water make me enter
ah mist of astral belly oh Newtown rose soon vivid
                         tangle then orchard sweep
a star revert why content why religion peal why liquid hearth retroflex
bike America Ill license pause remedial lead bloc rudeness avast! daddy pining
rise all why patter meter period blank space
coming up for air how do you celebrate
          Eros until loss order beatific surrender
beaten surrender east of excess alone with tea set
south of boundary placebo

47

I wanna sweat
I want Sweden
Me too

I want Costa Rica
What I won't do for a nearby lake
Iguazu

when was it last you were recommendable
my hubris moist today without recourse leaning into past
storm brew hot in shade ass sweaty but I resist
Parañaque set company aghast
yeah Im sure we broke the law
murderous guitar local allegiance pause blank

it is dangerous even to open your image oracle synapse
luminescence empire appear fossil wreck
how long & hard fight to get clear
name English yours averted elastic blank space
rose hibernation untitle to grip you here chosen
rose haberdashery odyssey Mnemosyne ambient blank space

what would you do Saturday
lucidity refraction why other inflection chasten most
to be remiss without your rose vital guzzle
question aquiline romp lace envy siren
question day I sign English yours ascertain lexicon pause
comment detourne all siren I I audit

game we throw into rope sonnet no rarer peace
rose essay vanish why article negative morning on the lam
why sell refraction satin settle under decency
rose is a vast salon in a question reversal
question ordinance deduce graffiti as obscure visor
lexicon hat here equip to rose

streets through rusty cage like lottery acid
on destroyed feet everything you say think anyway
pause blank space

50

"Writers like you make terrible husbands."

51

Good faith, they ask

states of smart ass . couldnt carry a dirge only sate it
question extraneous manner at the start . appear inversion saint immense as

its easy to believe I can sing without largesse   soul immerse nuisance impudence infinitive
cadavers denude avid question   livid unto hands I divvy up between us

hello, St Mark! demure here, my tired person   simpering, keeling, numb devoid period
flotillas adamant to trace deliquescent membrane   pendulum lead zenith I'll redeem

                                        ailanthus

                                        voices roll

                        sequin to voice other song duel . others
                                why other voices waste less on

                winters are hardest Ill abandon pause   wanders
                so long as I wont commit to spreadsheet I as a vill

                        in these borders   front . a dose of wh
                                entrances the dawn stabilizes

                perceive us as Ill stick you upon request . you hea
                states of suntans! no habit under antichrist   . o

                & Daytona inquire irradiate where where on

                        name English yours, your yours

                thirst for destiny Ill know beside a haberdashery meado
        Ill reserve for whomever has a sentimental song invented sample

        Orfeo surrender to short sentence period then indentation of

equivalence invention pervade crepuscular article   ocular sepulcher vibrate
around us nude cajole heritage   consequent sortie voice undulate
          as digital then arid etch lean . gypsy song equine to consort
le so that original murder period insist. immense stare nonce happens to anticipate

s dig out soup equate to avid station Ill despair
original   all murderous period blank space name English

under evening curtain mean to impugn sestina
ain, I see . a lost quandary less aghast equate brand

y I essay double unto doubloon here
entrances transfiguration create rearview mirror I

rd exclamation spend inverse travel
vivid Samothrace! voice wreath adventure song

ne suspend the hour . in other temple flick wrist
may be   rose invent soar to Eros fine equation announce

w sing .   restless   simper   keel   numb
ness my haberdasher sign to an orphan

servitude

53

God, said the blood   at the bottom of sound

IN CASE OF GLASS ABANDONED BALLAD

This boat penetrated endlessly into the fog

Far farther the one who says hate
Close closer says love

Paul Éluard

dance unchained limn celestial elegy
turn around to leave urgent nights preterit bare
dance unchained INS celestial derive
auxiliary supine delay orange lace desire boils blank heist

·

Im staring down the barrel of an uncertain second half
against a maladroit lace recoil under table
tout lesser transformation sonnet possibility

longing lead by solitary disguise surely appears as hated infinity
all description of passage importune pneumatic pause blank space
what'll it take for a just agreeable mission to remain enduring here

clarity wisdom of dizzy youth

comeliness aid the fool

VOLTAS DISPASSIONATE

a victim of my dizzy youth
coelacanth hell rope assassin

these villains a list semaphore question bust open crystalline
down caballero boulevard my cancer restive in the desert
lexicon witch doctor dominion question incantatory

Im trying to tell you to let me lay down my arms
lexicon losing animal sight of acid bath tower
De Legazpi's imago, Louis France argue with the harpies

lexicon toad eloquent TNT unsanctioned sordid odometer
in the court of the dragon we lay out our case
trapeze acts under cannibal circus led by matadora horror

Grendel Grendel, galling evil Linnaeus, Megton Gasgan irritant
a victim of own dizzy rope-a-dope gin rummy

De Legazpi's imago decrees:

RED INSECTS KILL

or

INCEST HANGS IN THE BALANCE!

boys in skirts circumcised within treason

~~Ill cut you down~~   ~~cellular rope~~

Acquiesce to me, adjacent novice delimit deity
no fair Verona to inter, a soul set to loose room
these are all my friends . Im perfectly certain they'll be

nice
to you too. No lives to fear denizen lead querulous
rope lasts a day addiction mile . Lenient horizon
comes to tremble enact appetite like a little lair
by the sea

Acquiesce to me, adjacent novice, sent to us in a seed
Verona blanks praise redolent or in a van. You are
from Las Piñas? Ill lead torsos into horticulture , a set of
venomous eunuch lunatics careful with incomprehension. Is
it light out already?
Rope sold in rinsed couscous

Acquiesce to me & Ill quell your adjacent delay .
One Ill sign trespass Lucifer rosy formidable
sullen toreador: matadora. Ha ha she'll

lead armor without a gem of Midas touch why frisky
memos in me . Invisible, shady brandish. A
secondary gong show to be sure . Ha ha ha—in a garden
surround soldiers with gust come living room saner
surrounding you disadvantage, Ill pulverize statues youth
congregate around , subsume
caskets of guardians silence under compress. So devoured .
Ill sit in salience surrounded by a base port, consul realized.
All the same Im pecking your age misery

No impregnable army necessary.   He who visits me succeeds
an elastic under Tuscan cuisine U.S. encounters in
set of vaccines , hay naku! Under cholera each
one of us proud elites aerate singly. Gently, gently

enemy—my eyes & my white creatures bestride me

SOLDIERING ON LIKE THE DEVIL

….inter media

aquiline rose semiotics limned novice entrance siege

in face of brute despair Ive no aversion litany a lost set arrhythmia

I have you I know but for how long border to border borders in glove

you say this is our home yet won't list my name under owner stanza

neither fear design a sinister lead equate to rope oracle

liquid made you shrug article gloam dagger

whenever I sit down to chat your English comes up like a mountain peak

inside alley of fear leans a horizon equip treble I reorganize

synchronous common cabals here they vow & un   ramp period space

and confusing

aquiline rose here is my last will & testament moment.

environs Ill blanket pared down to drink about being born in Las Piñas

yeah I grew up there I wonder how this iceberg   en. But when I of letters starts at our line

how you keep spelling to me like that that I am in a great as you left for work

slept on the couch again you kiss me on the cheek nothing to do intravenous

each hour sleeker leads to reel set back and always wish

like the Devil hollow earth points shoot away on this way to only lunacy

soul rope incomprehensible equinox aluminum join put the focus back on the poor

Lincoln's keynote address as I walk to these past few months. I've impacted the tenor

seconds before reneging endurance sala. I will meet someone else. You tell yourself

aquiline roses this poem picks up whg a tough time in NY at semiosis in all cruelty

delay jacaranda in bloom once   am wondering what's going on. Lenient trespassing

under Saint of Roses amid repairs self . Like we were talking about unless doubtful

hesitancy known you yell clear night but not clean at all & yet

rotisserie undo sole properties in a cave dwelling konmen & banshees celebrate

bleed armor with genus I do frisk with manners in hand in one garden
undone soul gateless use comedian at a loss for reunions pause blank space

disadvantage poet to deceive! Lorca pulverized by views of
congregation why states must go in case of fire raise guardian silence
they can egregiously devour us pause blank space in situ
Ill only use trapeze bar consensual reality at that at that
All I miss will encompass the language conjured by this poem
You pick & choose your moment to remind me of a house that's ours

I live in a rogue state one pregnant army advances . They visit cause
led by an emperor crustacean surrounded by buskers who use cursive
to encounter useless vaccination poem not name English yours there is
a dollar Hecate ropes Ill sing iridescence gently
can't escape the synchromystic creature on my shoulder
it's another year end with a film of a book by Tolkien
last time I caught it with you didn't lose its racism
before heat smash investment singularity

do I cue engine late in equine act once more, to lay low, hey
sing of Odin I thought it would be rouges here jamming, Tian Tian
darkness before dawn the color real emperor tomato ketchup

2

They come after me laterally like gilded lilies
Not you too in red dawn of New York City entity

once you named English yours

the ultimate rose

rogue rogue roses

quarter colors deed century

De Legazpi's imago la matadora catapult above houses

Alvin, I prefer the real yo to Louis' France

hurricane description plumb depths

bite English name it yours distress

equivocate protean Chaplin laser water powder satyr

3

SATURN ERUPTS

ATHENA

4

woke up & day just starting out
, me lookin so angry & be still is I feel
throttled

5

look at these books on the table to sell
in the jungle
another morning slept thru creep inside poem
over calm with storm wind across Angkor Wat
which you'll visit without me in October
maybe I feel dislodge whenever I sense
either one as far away & here
disguise myself

6

Im disguised as myself
law & order in New York tenement
quarter columbine design
own hurricane sample Negritude
de Sade for wear anguish in chapter
linen point to emotion Caspian friar
alone on a beach seal pups play
sway bodily new wave unease
I won't leave a moment like it

disguised as myself
red dawn New York give rope
purlieus parade in mansion with escalator
artist enter sala under burst of cascando
justice on the lam war foretell a jade Debussy

disguised as myself
your mouth ensure receipt all of Eden here
allegiance equip alliance no history mountain experience
collapse
furious enjambment nestle daemon advance
tall & drawn devour abandoned adieu

Im dis

    Im dis

disguised as myself solvent
empress shoestring conscious nonce paradise
of a morbid shed scour eyes harbor
how coyote signal forward plush relief
in my eyes takers market under century leaves
a soul lost juggernaut solace without art
a pseudonym absorption in song

                      disguised as myself
           a lesser sepulcher rope synecdoche radius
     you are Queen in this county impudence retrograde
        silence without sincerity rope loss barracuda
there are questions here equivocation to vacillating insouciance
        why linger in summit minute away from drop
       how come receiving satellites endure without
              frigate nor blood in the fridge
       sleep limn over hour delay day remnant
storm worm through gloaming in painted Angkor Wat

7

    What do you mean by "that devilish grin"?
no enemy staccato comeuppance ululation
cock excuse mauve abundance
are you a REAL Chinese

    pale day arose with laundry twenty minutes inside
still much to learn about sight Aztec difference I
learn to train regime equipoise to annealed ceiling
you unwrap gifts carefully then reuse spider web

Into solitude equivalent solemn hostile
utterance masquerade pure as Orthanc signpost
your silence marriage lead zenith Alsatian
woods keep a thermos of hot water for all time

its not paranoia smuggling these sybarite videos
what Caliban or Barabbas hasten chorus on cue
a map of days will lead you along estuary porpoise
demur Ovid while you hate to waste food

its where the engine of this poem lead you
I keep day unoccupied wake or strait of Im
Apollo's torso limit by rope Ill need to figure
normal armor identity, somber under Apollo

you save tinfoil & ziploc & grocery bag
alarm sound to remainder laundry lentil
consumer cuisine angle its sedentary
Tupperware usury carton rinse

kitchen of obscurity harbor turntable mystery
or elation by rope your wrists lead to bullets
once you said daddy looking back slow dive
night like it you'll never be alive press rewind

your collection of miniature shampoo
from hotels close down hearing to rim
maybe we're Nordic by nature
who show the part & brows

why must villainy shoulder us like the devil
when I kiss your open mouth this morning
laughter under sheets groan rescind noir engine adieu
rope surrender ruin telegraph fingertips fuel bus

why must villainy in the morning cloud angel head
saucy indices sever brevity perilous musk ache a lot
lets tighten this rose around wrist you insist saucy
indigo Nicean writ secondary century read zenith

you halve teacup with cover
when I ask to keep the glasses on
rose vowel first person heady bus race
rope loose ringtone feed you lengthen more

deep breath before the plunge
aubade sunlight lexicon dolor aid Apollo's torso
disguised as self ask if you've eaten of its midnight levee
Odin detain conqueror Herodotus Ill masquerade equilibrium

alligator lion alligator fury under shell
your parents boil herbs stay indoors when sick
may heal us if we seek it in the same way it desires
devour re-coup face sit fingertip pause blank space

alligator cavalier azaleas underwater Lorca
pulsate Eden nebula conjunction orator minutiae
toothpaste take squid paper-thin no routine
enemy anomaly pointillist English yours

just this stanza left
heady alacrity under-play Phaedrus must care
Louis' France stab troubadour swallow eye of fish
loss lost vestiges determine to murder shadow register

lament

edenic

aid hymn

Enoch

sky

handkerchief

wrote

8

sky   pierce   villain

WEEDING ANNIVERSARY

Im on fire

you know Im on fire when you come

closer yes here to beeline the drummer

these kids with blows & body odor mean well

think the way it is I like the sky a villanelle

our selves' cyclical Ill delay vessel anatomy

I figured it out amorous at eight Rome trammeled

ate eight no late umlaut tibia isn't intended

lead volta inured to a room envelope coursing

rope Ill fetch you infinity delay kissing lancer

your tough youth unto mezzanine in situ mezzanine

moving towards a clearing these years across wilderness

on a train my demure equality bubble liquid shell

I kissed your left shoulder glass full off hours

I caught a glimpse I made a vow figure out the difference

sang onto mezzanine your English mine I lower our bath set off & feet

DREAM ACHTUNG

a stab in the dark lose certain helices
wasted another morning of no name English yours
inquire rope Ill mount salad of Samothrace
a million miles of rope Ill mount delicious sojourn
lust heredity delicious manner
Florence rope Ill mount salad of universal dada song
to Judas

Florence rope Ill mount hour solipsism ballad under a billion atolls
a million miles rope Ill mount delay urgent sully Ill filter as blanket
inquire rope abandon taste of joy murder every anomaly lost periodical
so Danaë banned it

I course through Florence a mile of rope inquire stab troubadour
a lost train set enter a docent column blank space
a million miles salvation olive estate sequence renege
at royal harbinger tract
inquire asunder law homage Ill kneel manic sunless sojourn vacate
Deleuze's gypsy rose

Florence a million inquiries fear one less Nefertiti minus enemy anomaly

MONT BLANC

Im disguised as myself
with Job but not without
lore friends hearth family

did you see the chimp in the video
sign for the tourist to open the
latch of her enclosure

Im disguised as myself
there's mountain ranges in China
three somber decibels lower

certain passages of knavery
own Abyssinia Id soon sugarcoat
how many hours before the poem kicks in

Im disguised as myself
kneeling chant enchanted by hope
but they are protection

whenever the night steals its shadow
overcome by your sleep head
or your warm belly Im able to foster

like this disguise
purlieus Cimmerian child
siphon planet Ill badger with gallows

humor or taste apple pink
just a frail identity undone
own own my own

Im disguised as myself
stab lake three times mummification
countless masques delay inversion

castles Tintern Abbey question horizon
Ill appear questing restored in rucksack
light pollinate orb upon orb

disguised as myself Ill name English
yours enemy anomaly as prescient
lead villains to their doom

avuncular lodestar Offenbach decibel surrender Queneau's debtor
Le Morte d'Arthur antacid envisage walrus selfless inquire bet
sovereign voucher libraries forge Parmenides sell roaches as a sign
destiny my book legendary hostile shelling
lure sold rope imagine vast tripe conquest Parmenides lilied mane
Lorca in mid-February say mauve abundance embrace sudsy police
tempestuous delay, love

Nichiren is the difference. I weep & chant in the morning to see
science annul without anticipation
hour address English terrorist dissolve surfeit nude id paroxysm
it shouldn't be this coyote track teeth across belly
anxious elation butcher auxiliary paroxysm insouciant comedy
what I mean by this I lose your English name avuncular lodestar
etch in sky surrender roses

I see it like a pugilist dissolve double idea comment un-souse
palantir we hold up without dogged workout vale without similitude withdraw
dread beast to ignominious coyote howl moon along broadway wicker
I believe happen squander tornado or impasse wrong due pain
succor way detourne grenade oh no not this time
vows, beating, inquiry, as if all roses

settle more a dagger vision opera sully cochlea Ill eat luxury
why experience imagine loss of gendarme under roof bare like nexus offering
fumes . nouns. equate atoll against the grain . knot means to glisten
this poem occasion the end of time
not one bell , a trans person Circe offers trident
Lorca sings on a branch Moliere chance upon a lake
truffle sky commence guttural cheer latte in the city

re-adjust fine under normal medicine tuner

or equate I

magi

INSIDE COURT OF THE DRAGON

                    courtier to courtier deliver advance
                undrape trouser passage depend
              on beautiful silence grand nuance
                         equip to fate
                brute thaw

        courtier invite equate filial ride ring
              Cassiopeia
Escher to deliver advance   intense. It never
         rhizome doubt   one knows how to
cover or tout it   ve, make you feel
                  ter understanding
        poetry averted   major differences
Lavish estate behind amiable parents are pretty
Satan juice sovereign race made in their lives that
much in Venice   it were me, but I
lozenge said buckets   in situations…(just
                        navigate their lives has
        dust   Mostly in terms of things\
                less nit that's a whole nother
        flourish ur sister? I cant wait until
        agent of change   to spoil. Kids are the best.

STARFISH AORTA COLOSSUS

to Frank Lima

1

leaves the awash in desolate   I miss you under twisted rope where
I was on streets of rusty cage
oscillate sun-tossed room
what this week alike face of tornado cabinetry
brute thaw
this poem occasion the end of time
why experience imagine loss of gendarme under roof bare like nexus offering
I believe happen squander tornado or impasse wrong due pain
etch in sky surrender roses
Nichiren is the difference. I weep & chant in the morning to see
tempestuous delay, love
Lorca in mid-February say mauve abundance embrace sudsy police
siphon planet Ill badger with gallows
whenever the night steals its shadow

2

inquire asunder law homage Ill kneel manic sunless sojourn vacate
a million miles salvation olive estate sequence renege
a lost train set enter a docent column blank space
I course through Florence a mile of rope inquire stab troubadour
think the way it is I like the sky a villanelle
alligator lion alligator fury under shell
disguised as self ask if you've eaten of its midnight levee
from hotels close down hearing to rim
storm worm through gloaming in painted Angkor Wat
red dawn New York give rope
own hurricane sample Negritude
over calm with storm wind across Angkor Wat
hurricane description plumb depths
not you too in red dawn of New York City entity

darkness before dawn the color real emperor tomato ketchup
all I miss will encompass the language conjured by this poem
congregation why states must go in case of fire raise guardian silence
inside alley of fear leans a horizon equip treble I reorganize
in face of brute despair no aversion litany a lost set arrhythmia
rope lasts a day addiction mile. Lenient horizon
to you too. No lives to fear denizen lead querulous
in the court of the dragon we lay out our case
dance unchained limn celestial elegy
entrances the dawn stabilizes
winters are hardest Ill abandon pause   wanders
its easy to believe I can sing without largesse
soul immerse nuisance impudence infinitive
voices roll
streets through rusty cage like lottery acid

storm brew hot in shade ass sweaty but I resist
coming up for air how do you celebrate
ah mist of astral belly oh Newtown rose soon vivid
tell me, love, pondering the leaves
where cold can't recover itself
I leave you
in cold cold ocean
enter dialect ocean seismic Port Said
lean into salvation innocence
beside the beach you take me to watch baby seal pups
hunker down turquoise drop
why do I experience precious time as spend
boom boom water huh a pocket imbibe orphan tongue regurgitate
sepulcher coupling my window mitigate solaris

listless mist, carried, at last, at last, windowless
in my state of inquiry I base Eden near a lake
serpent inimical Colossus solo entomb mania excerpt
consensual. docent. escalator scalded in horizon enter frustration , hours
contract solemn obstacle ecstatic
let's be adieu or platelet of tungsten calm
there's no fight you can't fight   require ocean
the green will eat you
ah ah sunless   cadastral column echo
levee mass stank barren
pause rinse noon call rage orgone
at some point Ill need to go but not before I listen to the ocean
same day hours go to spend city sunken
the brown kid at last to be continued batten

6

despair yes lip service astronaut cord acquire pause
steeple terror hold you close when I sleep
spirit hawk low across cliff
can we speak tomorrow I mean this morning later tonight
past tense of inside
it will end in tooth if put to wrist like beach
seeking hell
instead of heading into the bleak evening
sit down for gongyo in fool compassion
sing record of enduring fiber
solid calm repose under shrug nerve ending
why wouldnt you go out on deathbed
Ive come back from the dead vegetal sordid
how to equip self

7

like stone tread underwater churn to flee
you'll drown inexperience swim
to swim but in pants shot punctuate what learn you
determine to swim further downhill large pirate sail
here we are on paper boat sail down flood walk
plan to meet on a boat but no clear idea what meander
get leaves behind in open living space
cry out name of anyone close to me in their strangle house
if only I could be green as you
justice or just fine or Pliny's ecstasy
you get to a point in mind & body when the eight winds don't sway you
oh something like lute in the grain
August comes to rock corollaries to coral reefs a saintly Capitan Tiago anoynymity
adjust equinox present painful exit grandeur cabal nuance Didn't I

8

verdure, esteem, hell, creation detain, despair why an ill-conceived panorama
knuckle 'em five seconds to vertiginous inamorata deicide Lethe minute rainstorm
mind before restlessness construction gavel police siren breeze
may day impossible for those who can't forget bereave nor afford pay out of
sky pumice decoration zone adieu
jelly of punitive decoration under zone rancid decay
like article of time passage alley under lost city eyes
terror portent allay
like an article of time passage in alley under lost city eye bear volcano
will October revolt against the uncanny wish-maker
do these to selves
empty beach Ive come to ruminate fear I thwart
name anguish mine
in truth Id fade in the mist of your stronger existence

rose rose ruin why trope Circes Ill denote linear columns
decay somewhere else, some nonce easily lost
a nude storm prima facie illusion for everyone , divinity
maybe October Ill see you pincer assume hazard tear
poet the ocean secret listening party inside hyena knowledge
calamity nadir shoulder naivety need signature discovery
flood eternal armor Inca tangle in the hour
grime inside hemisphere head of consulate indentation
inquire into October distance ocean initial chase
maybe of week distend ocean bodhisattva temple asleep
reminder to cross ocean no one hears
what are you doing this hour weather temporal
maybe I am wrong to seek out divinity
melody in ice bearing volcanoes cities envelopes

today it is no longer cry but admit yesterday I never once thought it
again tears call to the door begin to fall on the board of twenty
green inside languor wonder emergency the poem
wind sprint arrival are you
appear before blank space
name English mine divinity empty beach
on that empty beach we sit close to keep warm
live krakooom empty beach seal pups play while panda submerge
ocean bottom hearth buffet alien lane wide horizon
he comes calling like a shovel sign above sunlit tundra
I can will may know pen movement sling intention under starfish aorta
hurricane crescendo or catfish city sublimate English
name English tide return furtherance qua divinity
terror lament volta inquire why horizon aorta colossus impeach

11

Sign dwindle ghost divinity scansion tear heel algae heyday
In the morning rain canopy branch tongue finger climb
Entrances dawn stabilize tomorrow yesterday arrival everyday
Flood levity True Buddha no way but each bead
Maybe heaven before frontier clear
Leap out the moment they seize on the serpent
Fall water equipoise sketch
Prophetic   prosthetic   pathetic
Letters clatter equinox nonce consequence
Line you draw on ocean bed solstice in the Andes
Why   somebody   at sea   another mood
Key of cemetery music question endure war of the worlds
Devolve into passenger tsunami, a mise-en-scene too
Every inch towards Colossus

12

North Star nuance seat rope equinoctial season
why sing ocean multiply into imperial territory
season of shark Suetonius alleluia hush meow
yeah death parade train nonce to herald lost Genesis
cleave condition horizon chorizo etcetera dilettante
sink so low I even blame the sun
a bottle couldn't hope to survive the ocean, dilettante agreement melee
I get so excited when I write, excitable like squid plankton liquidity
in the tidal junction   , tidal as seismograph of balsamic track
receding states in the twilight whisper tales of murder
parables to be soused by at the turn of the tide
days look over shoulder for crustacean horizon
o useless I ocean lore cognate Im a quivering rose
stone of a gentle hunchback

IN CASE OF GLASS ABANDONED BALLAD

your tenuous unhinged question sell me a balloon like June eighteen
what this week alike face of tornado cabinetry
your tenuous moon hinge
synchro mystic date & condition force our nature to re-align hope yeah misterioso
say purlieus parade rose lore sacaren wheat arcane moon vertiginous detourne
oscillate sun-tossed room
I was on streets of rusty cage
lowering jugular unless similitude scale a leaden rose Ultima Thule
atoll of heart eschatology scabbard one cubit ode how jolly
attention lean corzine roundelay
didn't know Id hear from moon again nor am I chase become hope for nexus signifier
sacaren wheat field
half in the other room stew over who knows but yeah
here gulps are due lost altitude Im hinged Im hinged Im hinged
suddenly lowering jugular to a fragment about tidal whose trip to P.I. wow the future
sample equation patina under galleon pourings progress . Each train delay a moon
why lugubrious shoe dig the streets into walk, or shrink treeline comprehension
minion erase under pretzel wasn't much of sea algae unless caryatid
I miss you under twisted rope where   leaves the awash in desolate
your tenuous moon at nine
I always felt you were ready for me, baby
but I never plan for the worst do we all the best dress well
your tenuous moon pretzel to room bad jokes or take the J
it feels good to receive some writing from you
young tenure under Mars. Under question said Niobe. Under Mars.
Ive said too much already but this lost notice submit carton of salt companion
appear less fruitful attendant gush years why sell cereal attendant chupacabra
Im hearing self ask you outright say companion your sojourn rescue yesterday
around where abandoned ballad can least cope to assuage delay grimace

I want it determines
vow lesser chance anemone
lead offertory at the contrary road—corzine hearing o mien o might
jubilate Orfeo se intorno Eurydice pastorella ruby o coyote
Ive been direct & pure in procession that night with you more than anyone
in Lightland
just ask Khlebnikov—squandering the mess of my sacerdotal leviathan Ill mull over why
buoy consciousness in furtive brass
remarkable passage time no language subscribe to a line exclamation
appear a sprinter delicacy lead suggestion patina soul sapling nocturne rondeau
lost in helices
your tenuous moon reply one hinge suzerain Aetna gigabyte pause blank space
why wouldn't you nightly respond to query about own mother safety
why privilege the social death song sample ferocity why half of other devouring Pegasus
under ceiling of Paris

send me a child huddled beside a wet dog
you know temerity a sigil of laced cinnamon
I want to know Durer from your mouth at the tip of the pyramid this poem cut no lustral
visit Ill marry your autumn
solstice color bowl
appear serious to fornicate why Herod rope all leopard sold to regiments
sing to me, child, a hubris beside no sun under exclamation

Im involved there. Sober as Easter loneliness. Endure apparition witness to Orfeo
delicacy ghost music
yes Im a cobra bent enemy conjure Unamuno
present being what feeling no sight sounding touch following
like you said what's the point about nowhere—rope entrance coyote dense Ill center
delay mystery youth romping will antinomy
don't you at all experience remorse need attach human transfix gravity
ventricle Ill pilfer to Phaedra like locution
no more retro transistor radio under beautiful awhile white shirt

126

harangue canteen half of other atrophy couch butter

thrown off week somber as ambrosia waiting for the rest of time your left hand

slip along right no scab peeling

Ill tender one entry unhinged

Unhinged! Under heat! How did you know

Erasmus equal Osiris rope equivocate erasure unhinged

use Hygeia once Hygeia our child in song your goodbye furthers along

kay SAYA

ACKNOWLEDGMENTS

Poems in *Court of the Dragon* first appeared in recent volumes of *West Coast Line*, *The Capilano Review*, and *Vanitas*, as well as in the chapbook *Oh Sandy! A Remembrance* (Rail Editions) and the anthology *The Sonnets: Translating and Rewriting Shakespeare* (Telephone Books). Shouts to the editors and curators: Jeff Derksen, Sarah Dowling, Vincent Katz, Charles Bernstein, Phong Bui, Sharmila Cohen, and Paul Legault.

Higanteng pasasalamat din kina: Alex Tarampi and Toni Simon, for your haunting and unforgettable cover images; Alan Clinton and John Keene, for your kind words; Lindsey and HR, for your brilliant edit and design; Ma&Pa, Ninang, Mader, Trish, Eric, Tom, Despo, Sukhdev, Lucille, David, Courtni, Lucian, Emmy, Adrienne & John, Eds, Atul, Fred, Richard, Sigmund, Karl, Jill, and all Hokkeko-shu, for your camaraderie, wisdom, and compassion.

Most of all, I am grateful to Stephen Motika, champion of *Court of the Dragon* from the-get; and to my queens, Serena and Saya, who summoned it.

ABOUT THE AUTHOR

Paolo Javier served as the Queens Poet Laureate from 2010 to 2014. He is the author of seven chapbooks and three full-length collections of poetry, including *The Feeling Is Actual*, *60 lv bo(e)mbs*, and *the time at the end of this writing*, which received a Small Press Traffic Book of the Year Award. He edits 2nd Ave Poetry, and lives with his family in New York City.

ABOUT NIGHTBOAT BOOKS

Nightboat Books, a nonprofit organization, seeks to develop audiences for writers whose work resists convention and transcends boundaries. We publish books rich with poignancy, intelligence, and risk. Please visit nightboat.org to learn more about us and how you can support our future publications.

The following individuals have supported the publication of this book. We thank them for their generosity and commitment to the mission of Nightboat Books:

Elizabeth Motika
Benjamin Taylor

In addition, this book has been made possible, in part, by grants from The Fund for Poetry, the National Endowment for the Arts, and the New York State Council on the Arts Literature Program.